THE BIG DIPPER

THE BIG

DIPPER

by Franklyn M. Branley

Illustrated by Ed Emberley

THOMAS Y. CROWELL COMPANY • NEW YORK

LET'S-READ-AND-FIND-OUT BOOKS

Special Adviser: *DR. ROMA GANS*, Professor Emeritus of Childhood
Education, Teachers College, Columbia University.

Editor: *DR. FRANKLYN M. BRANLEY*, Coordinator of Educational
Services, American Museum—Hayden Planetarium, consultant on
science in elementary education.

1   2   3   4   5   6   7   8   9   10

THE BIG DIPPER

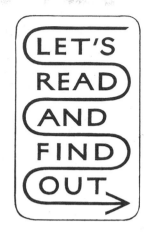

LET'S READ AND FIND OUT

I like to go outside at night.
Everything is still and dark.
At night I can see the stars.

Some nights the stars are very bright.
They look close, too. It seems that I can
    almost touch them.
I know I cannot. They are too far away.

My father and I look at the stars. We look at them
   in summer and in winter.
They are not always the same.

In summer, these are the stars I see.

In winter I see these stars.

But there are some stars that I can see
   both in summer and in winter.
I can see the Big Dipper whenever the sky is clear.

Long ago people drank water from dippers.
The Dipper in the sky looks like a water dipper.
It has a bent handle. It even has a bowl.

There are three stars in the handle of the Dipper.

There are four stars in the bowl.

I can see the Big Dipper in summer and in winter.
So can other people in the United States.
So can people all around the world.
The Big Dipper is always in the northern sky.

A compass points to the north.
The compass helps me to find the Big Dipper.
I hold a compass in my hand. I look in the direction
   that the compass needle points.

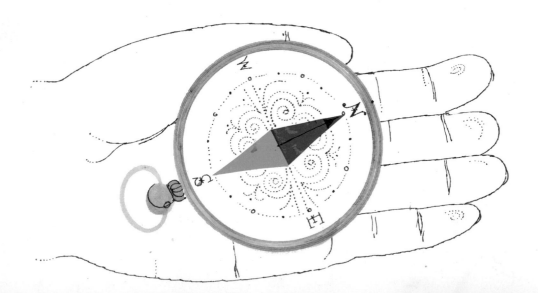

Sometimes the Big Dipper looks like this.

At other times it looks like this. But there are always three stars in the handle, and four stars in the bowl.

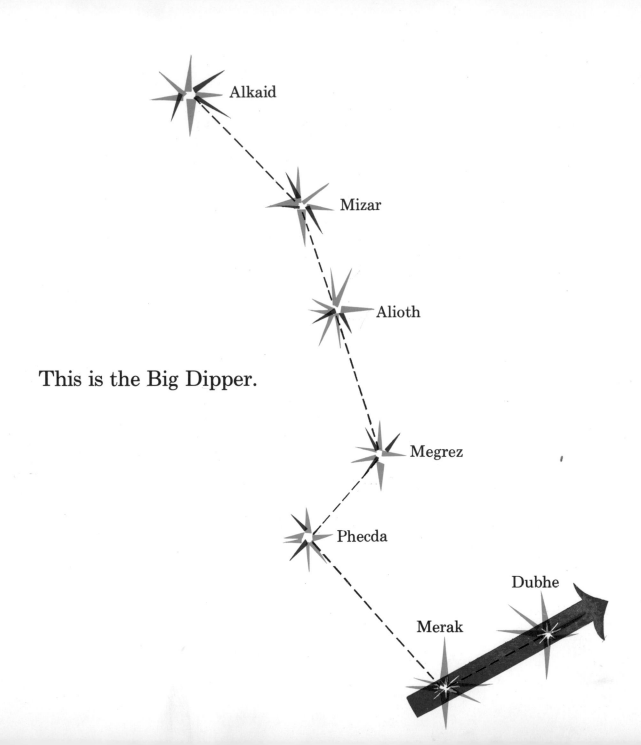

This is the Big Dipper.

Look at the two stars at the end of the bowl.

They are called the pointer stars because they point
to the North Star.

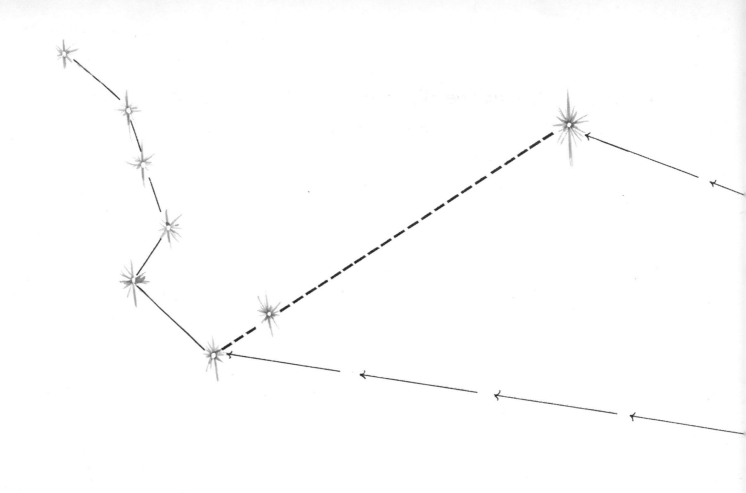

When you look at the Big Dipper in the sky, imagine a dotted line going from one star at the end of the bowl to the other one. Imagine that the dotted line goes all the way to the North Star.

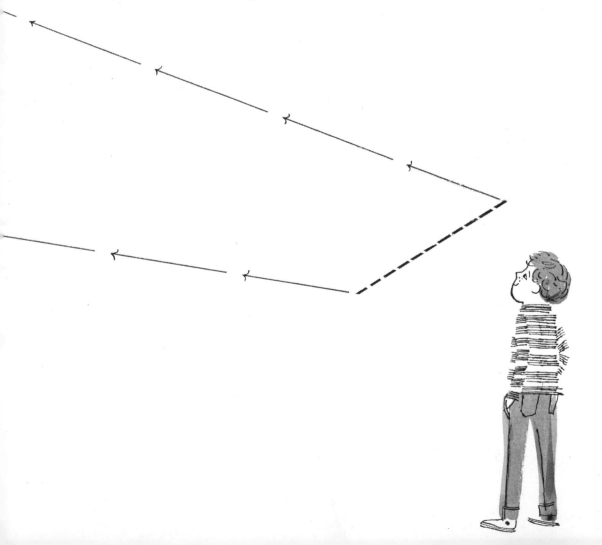

The North Star is a very important star.
Sailors use it to find their way.
They keep looking at the North Star. It tells them
which way they should sail.

The North Star is the first star in the handle of the Little Dipper. The Little Dipper has seven stars too. Whenever I see the Big Dipper, I can find a Little Dipper.

Why don't you look for the Dippers?
When the sky is clear and dark, go outside.
Look to the north. There you will see the Big Dipper,
    the North Star and the Little Dipper.

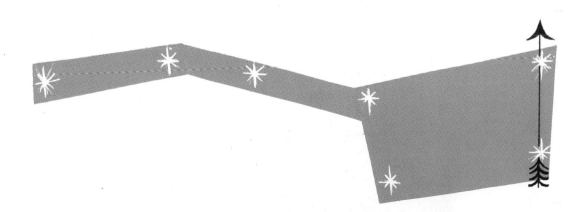

Long ago people imagined that the Big Dipper was
    part of a big bear.
They believed that the handle of the Dipper was the
    tail of the bear.
Four pairs of stars were the paws of the bear.
A bright star was his nose.

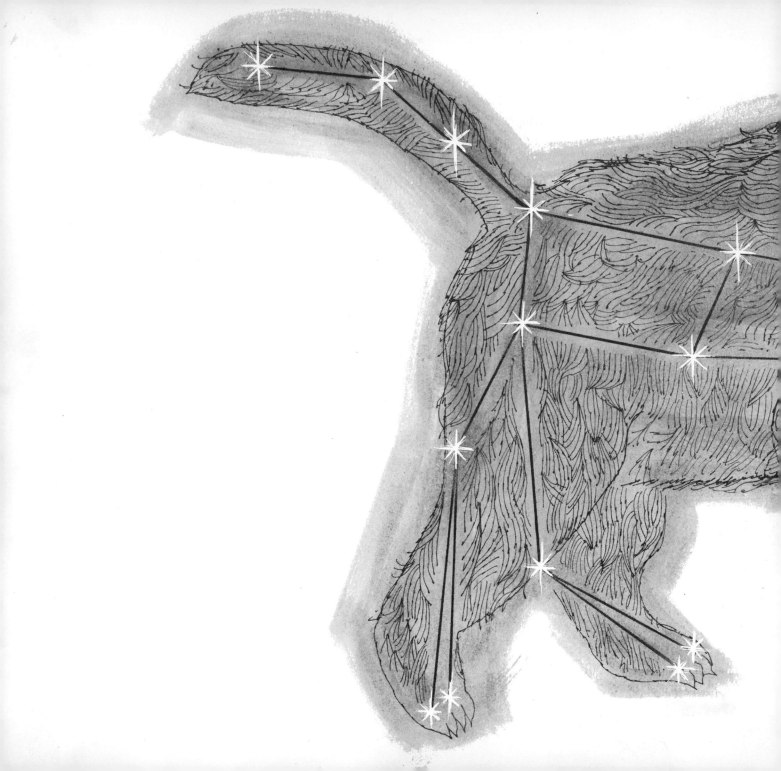

Sometimes I imagine that I can see
   the tail of the bear.
I make believe that I can see his head,
   and his nose, and his four feet.

People of long ago thought that the Little Dipper was
   part of a little bear.

I try hard to imagine that I can see the little bear,
   but I cannot.
Perhaps you can.

Some night when it is still and dark, take a friend
  outside.
Show him how to find the Big Dipper, the Little
  Dipper, and the North Star.

See if he can imagine that he sees the big bear.
Maybe he'll even be able to see the little bear!

ABOUT THE AUTHOR

Franklyn M. Branley is Associate Astronomer at the American Museum—Hayden Planetarium, where he has contact with audiences of all ages and where he directs the diverse educational program. For many years he has helped children learn scientific facts and principles at an early age without impairing their sense of wonder about the world they live in. Before coming to the Planetarium, Dr. Branley taught science at many grade levels, including the lower elementary grades, high school, college, and graduate school.

Dr. Branley received his training for teaching at the State Teachers College in New Paltz, New York, at New York University, and Columbia University. He lives with his wife and two daughters in Woodcliff Lake, New Jersey.

ABOUT THE ILLUSTRATOR

When he is not writing or illustrating, Ed Emberley pursues some interesting hobbies. He prints limited editions of children's books on his own hand press, studies Early Americana, and experiments with toy-making.

Mr. Emberley received a B.F.A. in illustration from the Massachusetts College of Art in Boston. He lives in Beverly, Massachusetts, with his wife and two young children.